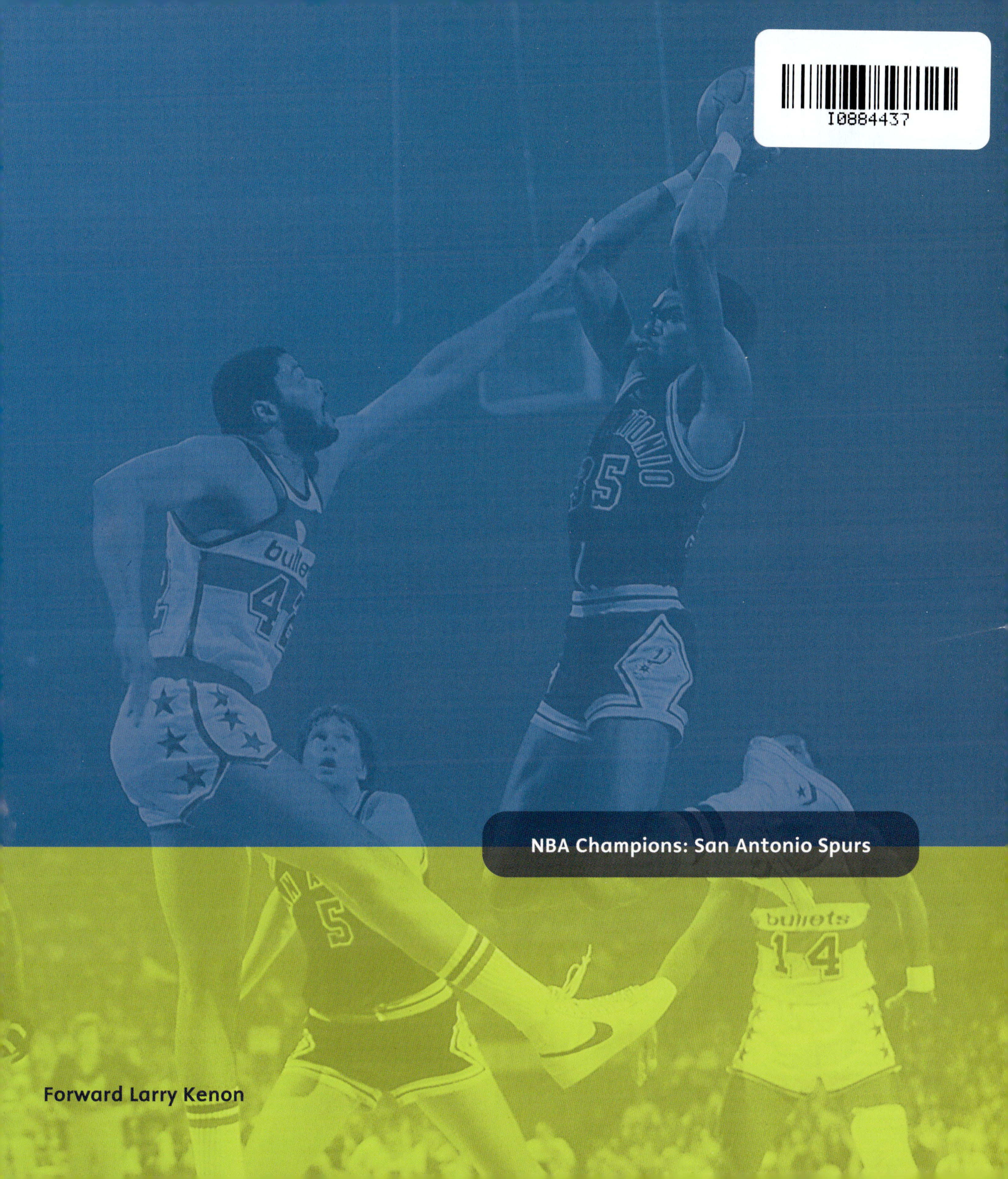

NBA Champions: San Antonio Spurs

Forward Larry Kenon

Center David Robinson

NBA CHAMPIONS

SAN ANTONIO SPURS

DENNY BULCAO, JR.

CREATIVE SPORTS

CREATIVE EDUCATION / CREATIVE PAPERBACKS

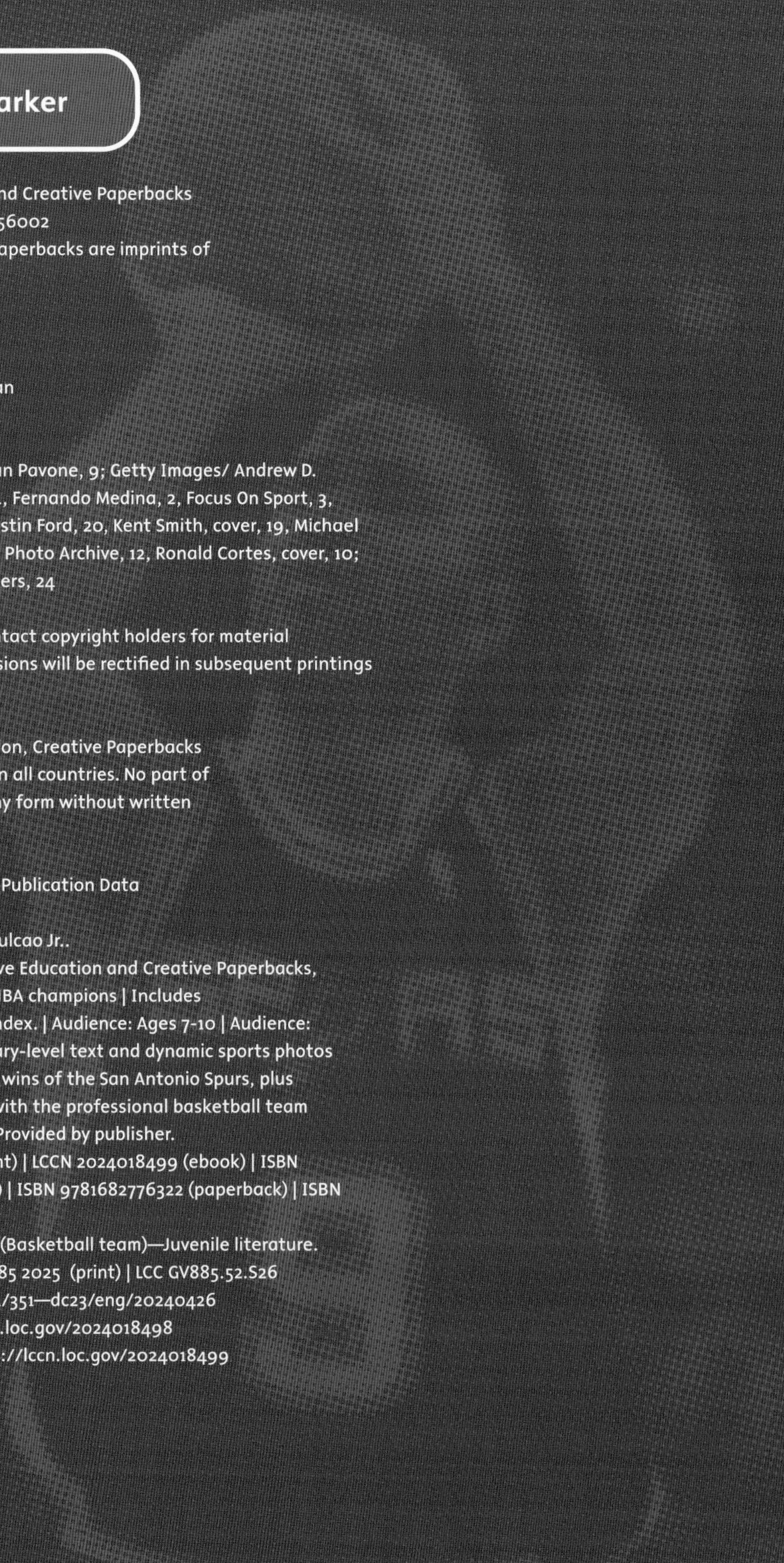

Guard Tony Parker

Published by Creative Education and Creative Paperbacks
P.O. Box 227, Mankato, Minnesota 56002
Creative Education and Creative Paperbacks are imprints of
The Creative Company
www.thecreativecompany.us

Art Direction by Tom Morgan
Book production by Graham Morgan
Edited by Grace Cain

Images by Alamy Stock Photo/ Sean Pavone, 9; Getty Images/ Andrew D. Bernstein, 6, Christian Petersen, 4, Fernando Medina, 2, Focus On Sport, 3, James Drake, 1, John Iacano, 15, Justin Ford, 20, Kent Smith, cover, 19, Michael Hickey, 5, Rocky Widner, 16, Rogers Photo Archive, 12, Ronald Cortes, cover, 10; Mark Sobhani/ZUMA Press, 7; Reuters, 24

Library of Congress Cataloging-in-Publication Data
Names: Bulcao, Denny Jr. author.
Title: San Antonio Spurs / Denny Bulcao Jr..
Description: Mankato, MN : Creative Education and Creative Paperbacks, [2025] | Series: Creative sports. NBA champions | Includes bibliographical references and index. | Audience: Ages 7-10 | Audience: Grades 2-3 | Summary: "Elementary-level text and dynamic sports photos highlight the NBA championship wins of the San Antonio Spurs, plus sensational players associated with the professional basketball team such as Victor Wembanyama"— Provided by publisher.
Identifiers: LCCN 2024018498 (print) | LCCN 2024018499 (ebook) | ISBN 9798889892663 (library binding) | ISBN 9781682776322 (paperback) | ISBN 9798889893776 (ebook)
Subjects: LCSH: San Antonio Spurs (Basketball team)—Juvenile literature.
Classification: LCC GV885.52.S26 B85 2025 (print) | LCC GV885.52.S26 (ebook) | DDC 796.323/64/09764/351—dc23/eng/20240426
LC record available at https://lccn.loc.gov/2024018498
LC ebook record available at https://lccn.loc.gov/2024018499

Printed in China

Forward/center LaMarcus Aldridge

Forward Robert Horry

CONTENTS

Home of the Spurs 8

Naming the Spurs 13

Spurs History 14

Other Spurs Stars 21

About the Spurs 22

Glossary 23

Index 24

Home of the Spurs

San Antonio is a large city in south-central Texas. Years ago, Texas wanted independence from Mexico. San Antonio was the site of the famous Battle of the Alamo in 1836. The city has an **arena** called the Frost Bank Center. It is the home of a basketball team called the Spurs.

Guard Patty Mills

The Spurs are part of the National Basketball Association (NBA). They play against other teams in the NBA. They try to win the **NBA Finals**. The Spurs' main **rivals** are the Dallas Mavericks and the Houston Rockets. They play in the Southwest Division of the Western Conference.

Guard George Gervin

Naming the Spurs

The team was first called the Dallas Chaparrals. A chaparral is a thicket of small trees or shrubs. The team's name changed to the Spurs when they moved to San Antonio. Ranchers in Texas sometimes wear spurs on their boots to control their horses.

Spurs History

The team began playing in 1967. They moved to San Antonio in 1973. They were renamed the Spurs. Guard James Silas helped the Spurs make the **playoffs**. A big fan favorite was George Gervin. They called him "Iceman" because he kept his cool when he played.

Guard James Silas

Center David Robinson

In 1989, 7-foot-1 center David Robinson came to the Spurs. The team picked up more star players. In 1997, they chose talented center-forward Tim Duncan. Robinson and Duncan helped the Spurs become NBA champions in 1999.

Coach Gregg Popovich led the Spurs to three more **titles** in 2003, 2005, and 2007. Quick guard Tony Parker made exciting plays. Lefty guard Manu Ginóbili was great at making creative plays and impressive shots.

The Spurs reached the Finals in 2013 but lost to the Miami Heat in seven games. The next year's Finals featured a rematch. The Spurs won their fifth NBA title by beating the Heat in five games.

Center/forward Tim Duncan

Center Victor Wembanyama

Other Spurs Stars

High-jumping forward Larry Kenon starred in the 1970s. Alvin Robertson led the NBA in steals for three seasons. In the 1990s, Sean Elliott made big shots. Tough forward Bruce Bowen was on the All-Defensive First Team five times in the 2000s.

Kawhi Leonard led San Antonio to a fifth championship in 2014. He was a top scorer and **defender**. He was named **Most Valuable Player (MVP)** of the 2014 Finals. Fans think young star Victor Wembanyama can lead the Spurs to another championship!

About the Spurs

First season: 1967—68

Conference/division: Western Conference, Southwest Division

Team colors: black and silver

Home arena: Frost Bank Center

NBA CHAMPIONSHIPS:

1999, 4 games to 1 over New York Knicks

2003, 4 games to 2 over New Jersey Nets

2005, 4 games to 3 over Detroit Pistons

2007, 4 games to 0 over Cleveland Cavaliers

2014, 4 games to 1 over Miami Heat

TEAM WEBSITE:

https://www.nba.com/spurs/

Glossary

arena—a large building with seats for spectators, where sports games and entertainment events are held

defender—a player who stops the other team from scoring

Most Valuable Player (MVP)—an honor given to the season's best player

NBA Finals—a series of games between two teams at the end of the playoffs; the first team to win four games is the champion

playoffs—games that the best teams play after a regular season to see who the champion will be

rival—a team that plays extra hard against another team

title—another word for championship

Center/forward Tim Duncan

Index

Bowen, Bruce, 21

Duncan, Tim, 17, 19

Frost Bank Center, 8, 22

Gervin, George, 12, 14

Ginóbili, Manu, 17

Kenon, Larry, 1, 21

Leonard, Kawhi, 21

Parker, Tony, 4, 17

Robinson, David, 2, 16, 17

Silas, James, 14, 15

team name, 13, 14

Wembanyama, Victor, 20, 21